# MACDONALD STARTERS

# Butterflies

## Macdonald Educational

W9-BSY-374

juv QL544.2 B884 1972

**About Macdonald Starters**

Macdonald Starters are vocabulary controlled information books for young children. More than ninety per cent of the words in the text will be in the reading vocabulary of the vast majority of young readers. Word and sentence length have also been carefully controlled.

Key new words associated with the topic of each book are repeated with picture explanations in the Starters dictionary at the end. The dictionary can also be used as an index for teaching children to look things up.

Teachers and experts have been consulted on the content and accuracy of the books.

**Illustrated by:** John Mousdale

**Editors:** Peter Usborne, Su Swallow, Jennifer Vaughan

**Reading consultant:** Donald Moyle, author of *The Teaching of Reading* and senior lecturer in education at Edge Hill College of Education

**Chairman, teacher advisory panel:** F. F. Blackwell, general inspector for schools, London Borough of Croydon, with responsibility for primary education

**Teacher panel:** Elizabeth Wray, Loveday Harmer, Lynda Snowdon, Joy West

© Macdonald and Company (Publishers) Limited 1972
**Second Impression 1973**
Made and printed in Great Britain by Purnell & Sons Limited Paulton, nr Bristol

First published 1972 by Macdonald and Company (Publishers) Limited
St Giles House
49-50 Poland Street
London W1

I can see a butterfly.
It is on a flower.

1

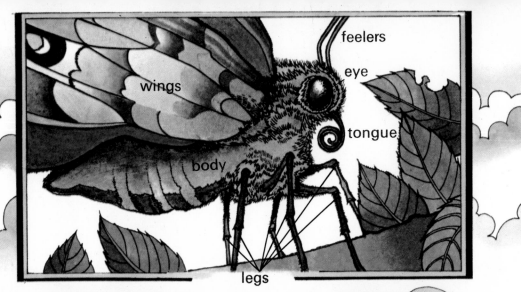

feelers

eye

wings

tongue

body

legs

forewings

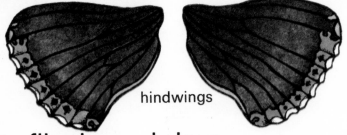

hindwings

Butterflies have six legs.
They have four wings.
The wings are often beautifully coloured.

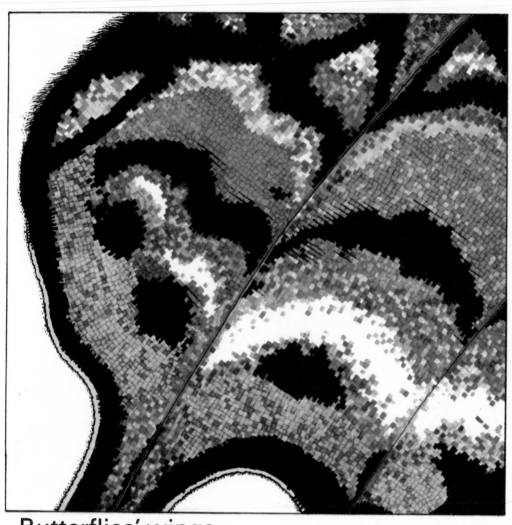

Butterflies' wings
have tiny scales all over them.
Each scale is coloured.
Together they make the pattern.

Most butterflies
drink nectar from flowers.
They have long tongues for drinking.

Female butterflies lay eggs.
They often lay them on leaves.

When the eggs hatch
caterpillars come out.
At first the caterpillars
are very small.

Most caterpillars eat leaves.
The caterpillars grow big.

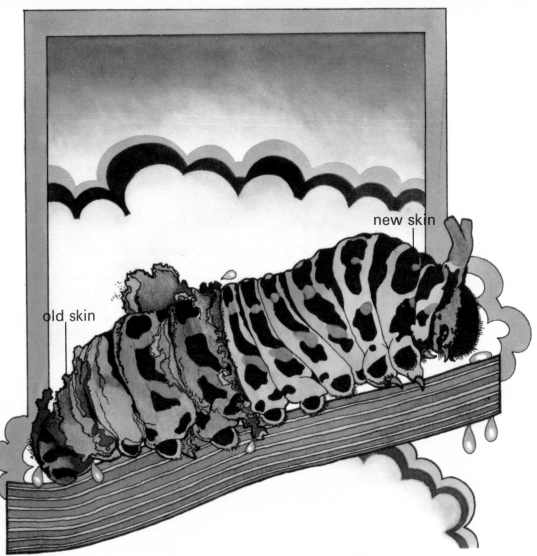

new skin

old skin

When the caterpillars grow big
they need a bigger skin.
The old skin comes off.
There is a new skin underneath.

8

The caterpillar makes
a hard case for itself.
Inside the case, the caterpillar
turns into a butterfly.

The butterfly comes out.
It spreads its wings
and flies away.

10

Brown Argus

Orange tip

Skipper

Swallowtail

Tortoiseshell

Blue

There are many kinds
of butterflies.
Here are some of them.

This butterfly
lives in a hot country.
It is very big.
It is called a Birdwing.
12

This white butterfly
is quite small.
It lays eggs on cabbages.
The caterpillars eat the cabbages.

These are Monarch butterflies.
They live in America.
They fly south in autumn.
They fly north in spring.

14

These are peacock butterflies.
They have patterns on their wings.
The patterns look like
the patterns on a peacock's tail.

Here are some moths.
Moths are like butterflies.
But their wings are different.
16

These caterpillars
will be moths one day.
They have made a big web to live in.
It is like a spider's web.

These moth caterpillars
live on trees in a wood.
There are too many caterpillars.
They have eaten nearly all the leaves.
18

These are clothes moths.
They lay eggs on clothes.
The eggs hatch.
The caterpillars eat the clothes.

Many moths fly about at night.
They often fly into lights.

20

Some moths fly about
in the day.
They are often beautiful colours.

21

## See for yourself
Find a caterpillar.
Feed it on the kind of leaves
you found it on.
Watch it grow up.
22

# Starter's **Butterflies** words

**butterfly**
(page 1)

**tongue**
(page 2)

**flower**
(page 1)

**body**
(page 2)

**legs**
(page 2)

**wings**
(page 2)

**eyes**
(page 2)

**scales**
(page 3)

**feelers**
(page 2)

**drink**
(page 4)

23

nectar
(page 4)

eggs
(page 5)

leaf
(page 5)

caterpillar
(page 6)

eat
(page 7)

skin
(page 8)

case
(page 9)

fly
(page 10)

Swallowtail
(page 11)

Birdwing
(page 12)

24

# Monarch butterfly
(page 14)

# Peacock butterfly
(page 15)

# peacock
(page 15)

# moth
(page 16)

# web
(page 17)

# spider
(page 17)

# tree
(page 18)

# wood
(page 18)

# clothes
(page 19)

# light
(page 20)

**D**

Brodart Co.                    Ca